Sing A Song Of Nursery Rhymes

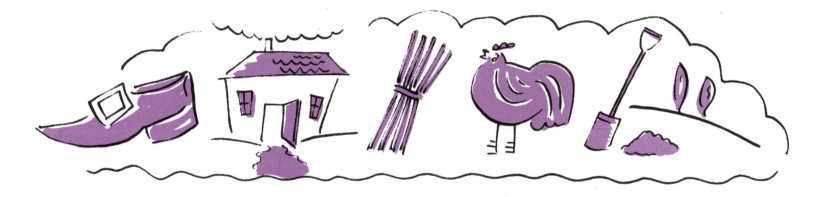

Mary Thompson

Illustrated by David Meldrum

Chester Music Limited

(A division of Music Sales Ltd.)
8/9 Frith Street, London W1V 5TZ

Contents

Humpty Dumpty	3	Baa, Baa, Black Sheep	21
Three Blind Mice	4	Old King Cole	22
Little Miss Muffet	5	Bye, Baby Bunting	24
Hickory, Dickory, Dock	6	Rub-a-dub-dub, Three Men In A Tub	25
Peter Piper	7	Simple Simon	26
Twinkle, Twinkle, Little Star	8	Sur Le Pont D'Avignon	28
See-saw, Margery Daw	10	What Are Little Boys Made Of?	29
Polly Put The Kettle On	11	One, Two, Buckle My Shoe	30
Little Polly Flinders	12	I Love Little Pussy	32
There Was A Crooked Man	13	There Was An Old Woman Who Lived In A Shoe	33
Old Mother Hubbard	14		
Frère Jacques	16	Yankee Doodle	34
Ding Dong Bell	17	This Little Pig Went To Market	36
Where Are You Going To, My Pretty Maid?	18	Tom, Tom, The Piper's Son	37
		Three Little Kittens	38
Oh Where, Oh Where Has My Little Dog Gone?	20	Sing A Song Of Sixpence	40

Cover design by Chloë Alexander
Printed and bound in the United Kingdom by
Caligraving Limited, Thetford, Norfolk.

Order No. CH61494   ISBN 0-7119-7529-9

Unauthorised reproduction of any part of this publication by any means
including photocopying is an infringement of copyright.

Three Blind Mice

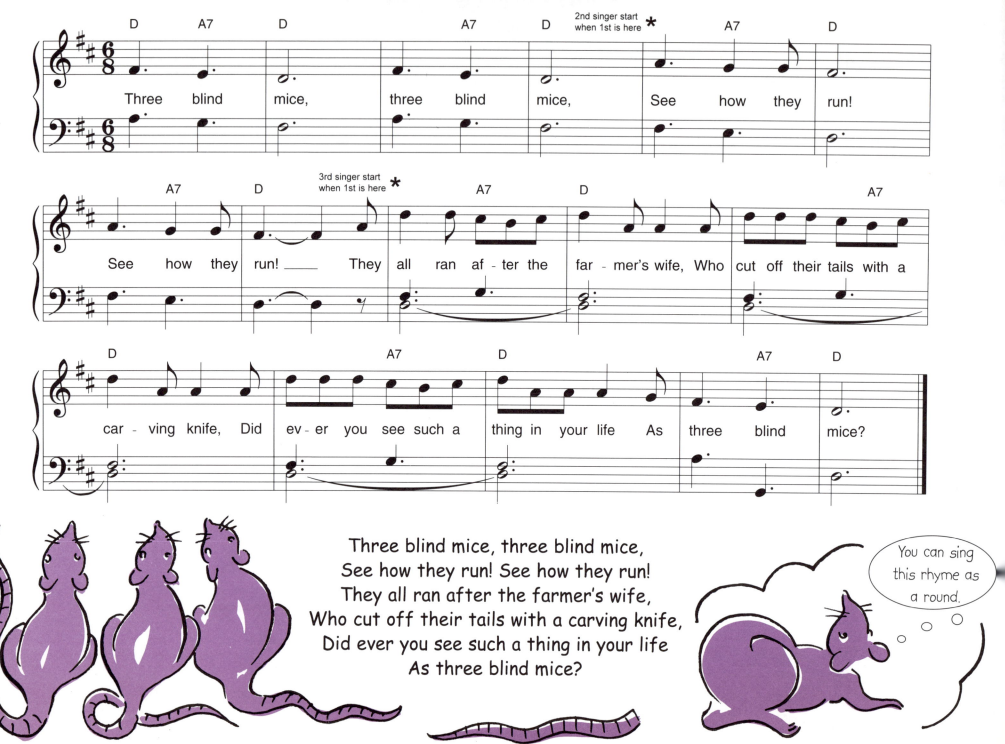

Three blind mice, three blind mice,
See how they run! See how they run!
They all ran after the farmer's wife,
Who cut off their tails with a carving knife,
Did ever you see such a thing in your life
As three blind mice?

You can sing this rhyme as a round.

Peter Piper

Peter Piper picked a peck of pickled pepper,
Peter Piper picked a peck of pickled pepper.
If Peter Piper picked a peck of pickled pepper,
Where's the peck of pickled pepper Peter Piper picked?

Twinkle, Twinkle, Little Star

1. Twinkle, twinkle, little star,
   How I wonder what you are,
   Up above the world so high,
   Like a diamond in the sky.
   Twinkle, twinkle, little star,
   How I wonder what you are.

2. When the blazing sun is gone,
   When he nothing shines upon,
   Then you show your little light,
   Twinkle, twinkle, all the night.
   Twinkle, twinkle, little star,
   How I wonder what you are.

3. Then the traveller in the dark
   Thanks you for your tiny spark.
   Could he see which way to go
   If you did not twinkle so?
   Twinkle, twinkle, little star,
   How I wonder what you are.

4. In the dark blue sky you keep,
   And often through my curtains peep.
   For you never shut your eye
   Till the sun is in the sky.
   Twinkle, twinkle, little star,
   How I wonder what you are.

This is often sung at bedtime, to help small children go to sleep.

See-saw, Margery Daw

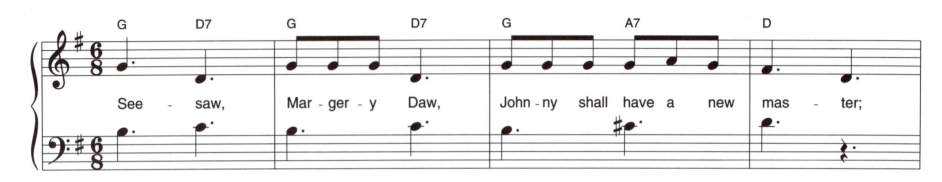
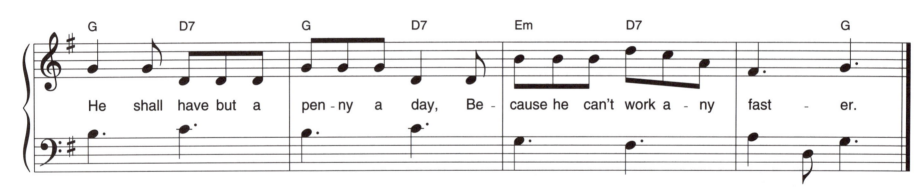

See-saw, Margery Daw,
Johnny shall have a new master;
He shall have but a penny a day,
Because he can't work any faster.

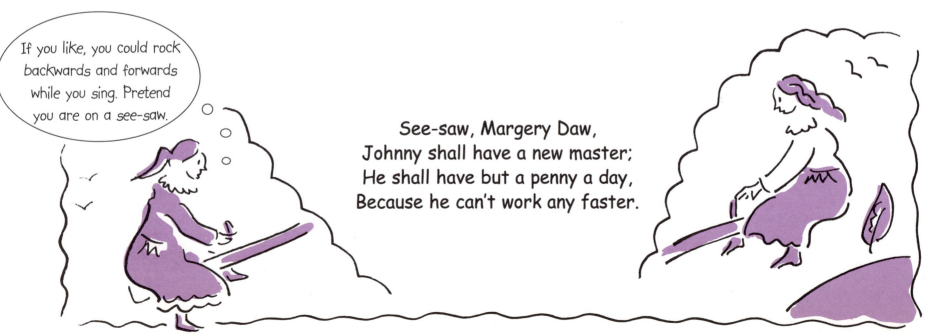

If you like, you could rock backwards and forwards while you sing. Pretend you are on a see-saw.

Little Polly Flinders

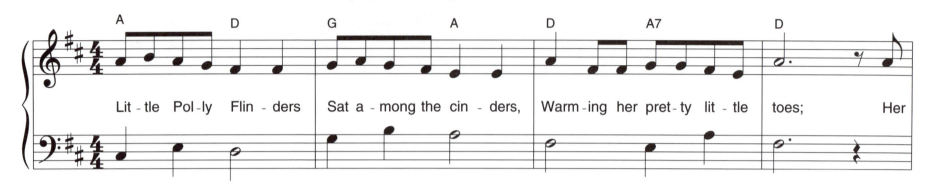

Cinders are the burnt bits of wood and coal left around a fire.

Little Polly Flinders
Sat among the cinders,
Warming her pretty little toes;
Her mother came and caught her,
And smacked her little daughter,
For spoiling her nice new clothes.

There Was A Crooked Man

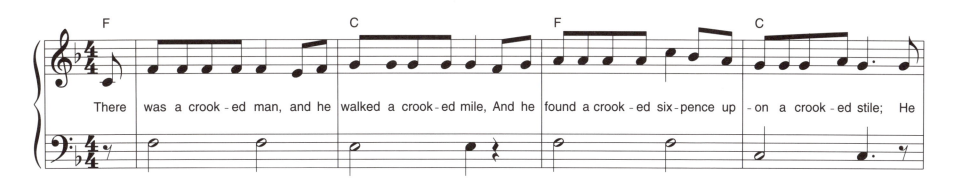

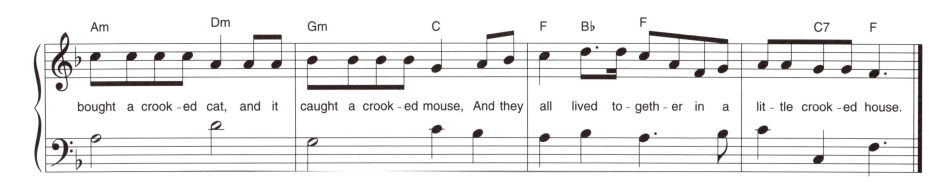

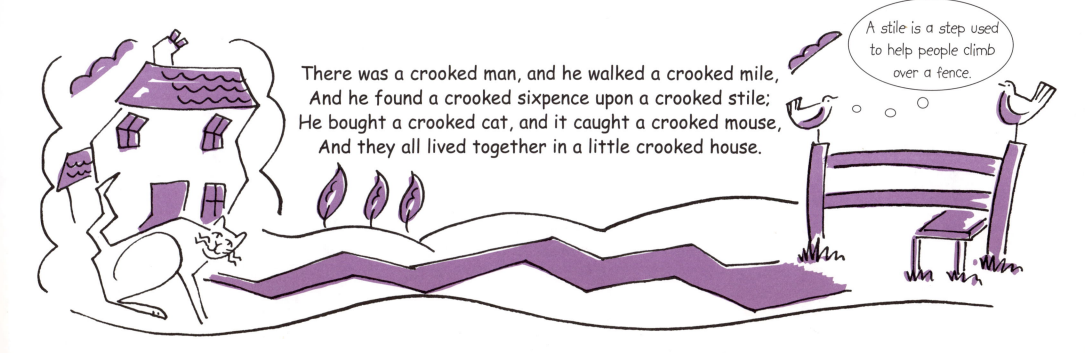

There was a crooked man, and he walked a crooked mile,
And he found a crooked sixpence upon a crooked stile;
He bought a crooked cat, and it caught a crooked mouse,
And they all lived together in a little crooked house.

A stile is a step used to help people climb over a fence.

2. She went to the baker's to buy him some bread;
   But when she came back the poor dog was dead.

3. She went to the undertaker's to buy him a coffin;
   But when she came back the poor dog was laughing.

4. She took a clean dish to get him some tripe;
   But when she came back he was smoking a pipe.

5. She went to the alehouse to get him some beer;
   But when she came back the dog sat in a chair.

6. She went to the tavern for white wine and red;
   But when she came back the dog stood on his head.

7. She went to the fruiterer's to buy him some fruit;
   But when she came back he was playing the flute.

8. She went to the tailor's to buy him a coat;
   But when she came back he was riding a goat.

9. She went to the hatter's to buy him a hat;
   But when she came back he was feeding the cat.

10. She went to the barber's to buy him a wig;
    But when she came back he was dancing a jig.

11. She went to the cobbler's to buy him some shoes;
    But when she came back he was reading the news.

12. She went to the seamstress to buy him some linen;
    But when she came back the dog was a-spinning.

13. She went to the hosier's to buy him some hose;
    But when she came back he was dressed in his clothes.

14. The dame made a curtsy, the dog made a bow;
    The dame said,"Your servant", the dog said, "Bow-wow".

Frère Jacques

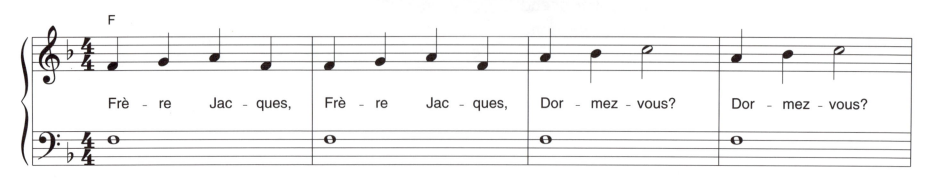

Frère Jacques means "Brother Jack".

Frère Jacques, Frère Jacques,
Dormez-vous? Dormez-vous?
Sonnez les matines,
Sonnez les matines,
Ding, dingue, dong,
Ding, dingue, dong.

Ding Dong Bell

Ding dong bell! Pussy's in the well!
Who put her in? Little Tommy Green.
Who pulled her out? Little Tommy Stout.
What a naughty boy was that to drown poor pussy cat,
Who ne'er did any harm,
But killed all the mice in his father's barn.

Where Are You Going To, My Pretty Maid?

1. "Where are you going to, my pretty maid?
   Where are you going to, my pretty maid?"
   "I'm going a-milking, sir," she said,
   "Sir," she said, "sir," she said.
   "I'm going a-milking, sir," she said.

2. "May I go with you, my pretty maid?
   May I go with you, my pretty maid?"
   "Yes, if you please, kind sir," she said,
   "Sir," she said, "sir," she said.
   "Yes, if you please, kind sir," she said.

3. "What is your fortune, my pretty maid?
   What is your fortune, my pretty maid?"
   "My face is my fortune, sir," she said,
   "Sir," she said, "sir," she said.
   "My face is my fortune, sir," she said.

4. "Then I can't marry you, my pretty maid?"
   "Then I can't marry you, my pretty maid?"
   "Nobody asked you, sir," she said,
   "Sir," she said, "sir," she said.
   "Nobody asked you, sir," she said.

Oh Where, Oh Where Has My Little Dog Gone?

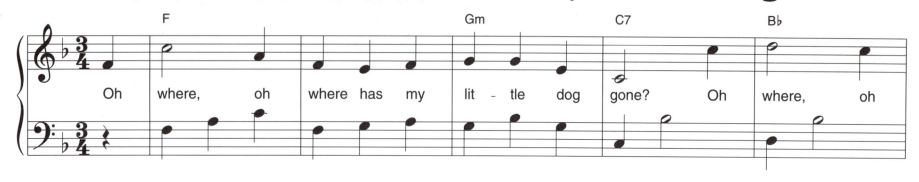
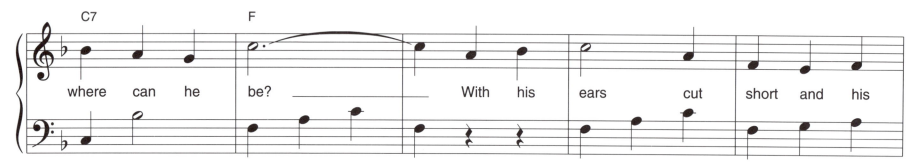

Oh where, oh where has my little dog gone?
Oh where, oh where can he be?
With his ears cut short and his tail cut long,
Oh where, oh where is he?

Old King Cole

A fiddle is another name for a violin.

Old King Cole was a merry old soul,
And a merry old soul was he,
He called for his pipe, and he called for his bowl,
And he called for his fiddlers three.
Every fiddler had a fiddle so fine,
And a very fine fiddle had he,
O there's none so rare as can compare
With King Cole and his fiddlers three.

Bye, Baby Bunting

Bye, Baby Bunting,
Daddy's gone a-hunting,
To get a little rabbit skin
To wrap the Baby Bunting in.

Sing this rhyme very quietly.

Rub-a-dub-dub, Three Men In A Tub

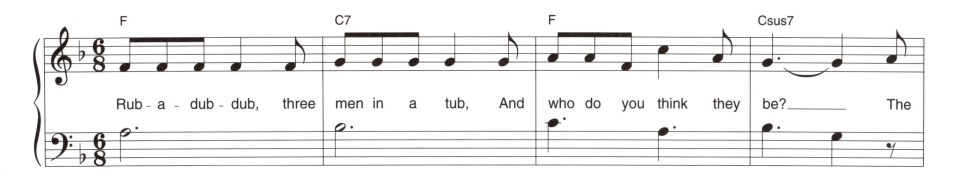

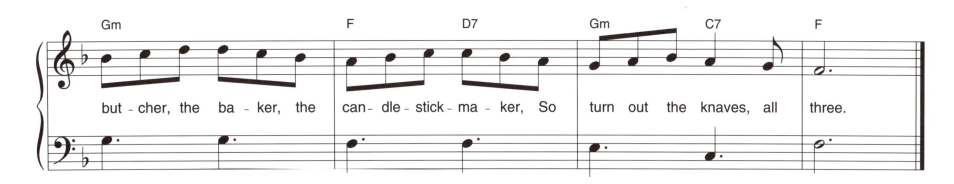

Rub-a-dub-dub, three men in a tub,
And who do you think they be?
The butcher, the baker, the candlestick maker,
So turn out the knaves, all three.

Knave is another word for a rascal.

Simple Simon

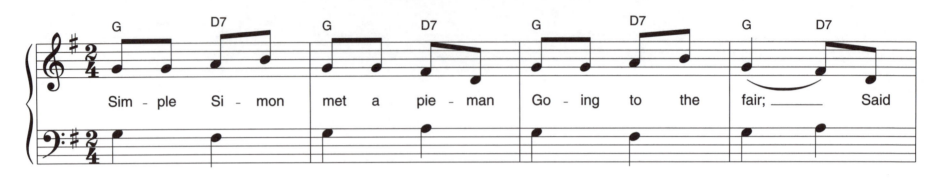

1. Simple Simon met a pieman
Going to the fair;
Said Simple Simon to the pieman,
"Let me taste your ware."

A pieman is someone who sells pies.

2. Said the pieman unto Simon,
   "Show me first your penny;"
   Said Simple Simon to the pieman,
   "Sir, I haven't any."

3. Simple Simon went a-fishing
   For to catch a whale;
   But all the water he had got
   Was in his mother's pail.

4. Simple Simon went to look
   If plums grew on a thistle;
   He pricked his fingers very much,
   Which made poor Simon whistle.

Sur Le Pont D'Avignon

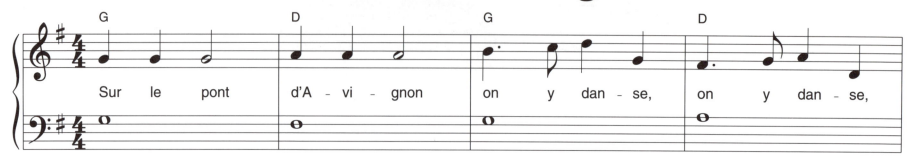
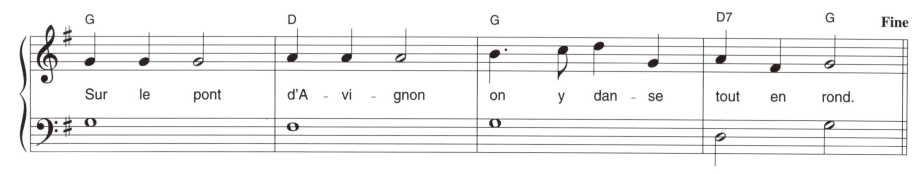
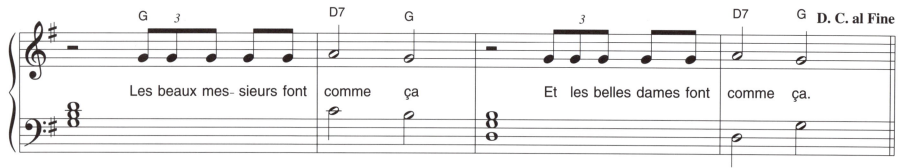

This rhyme is from France. The title means, "On the bridge at Avignon."

Sur le pont d'Avignon on y danse, on y danse,
Sur le pont d'Avignon on y danse tout en rond.
Les beaux messieurs font comme ça
Et les belles dames font comme ça.
Sur le pont d'Avignon on y danse, on y danse,
Sur le pont d'Avignon on y danse tout en rond.

What Are Little Boys Made Of?

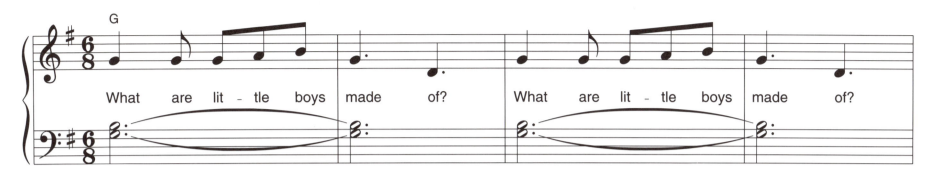

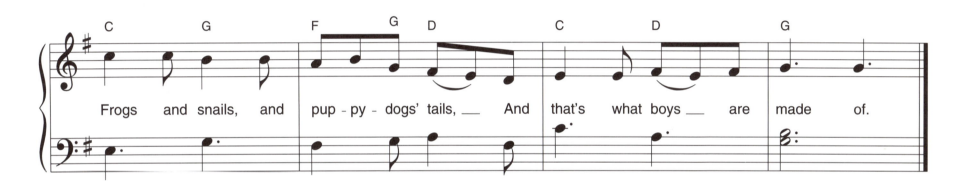

If you have a group of children, the boys could sing the first verse and the girls could sing the second.

1. What are little boys made of?
   What are little boys made of?
   Frogs and snails, and puppy-dogs' tails,
   And that's what boys are made of.

2. What are little girls made of?
   What are little girls made of?
   Sugar and spice, and all things nice,
   And that's what girls are made of.

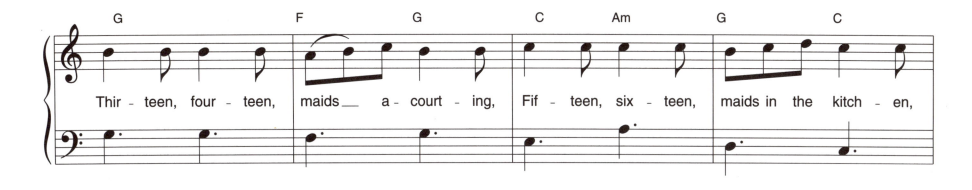
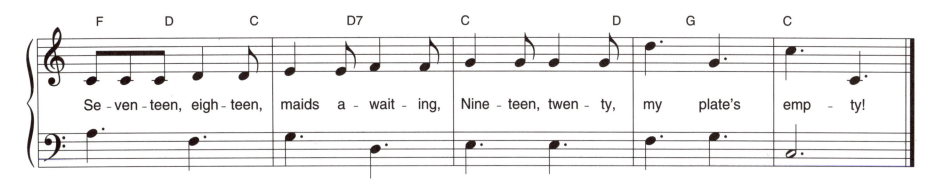

One, two, buckle my shoe,
Three, four, open the door,
Five, six, pick up sticks,
Seven, eight, lay them straight,
Nine, ten, a good fat hen,
Eleven, twelve, dig and delve,
Thirteen, fourteen, maids a-courting,
Fifteen, sixteen, maids in the kitchen,
Seventeen, eighteen, maids a-waiting,
Nineteen, twenty, my plate's empty!

I Love Little Pussy

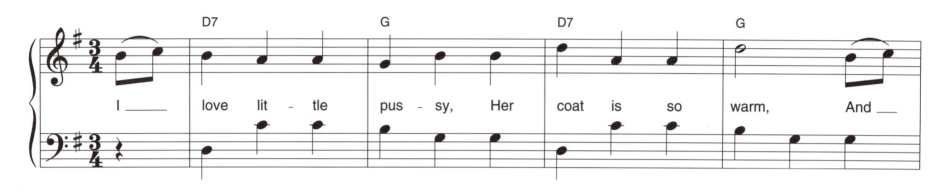

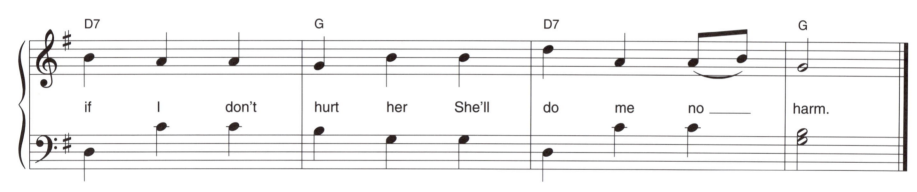

Sing this rhyme very gently.

1. I love little pussy,
   Her coat is so warm,
   And if I don't hurt her
   She'll do me no harm.

2. I'll not pull her tail,
   And won't drive her away,
   But pussy and I
   Together will play.

3. She'll sit by my side,
   And I'll give her some food,
   And she'll like me, because
   I am gentle and good.

There Was An Old Woman Who Lived In A Shoe

There was an old woman who lived in a shoe,
She had so many children she didn't know what to do;
She gave them some broth, without any bread,
Then she whipped them all round, and sent them to bed.

A long time ago, families were often much bigger than they are today.

Yankee Doodle

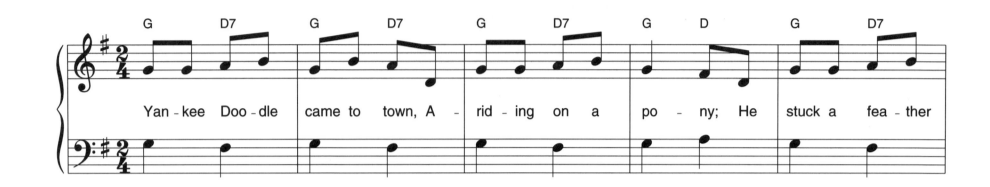

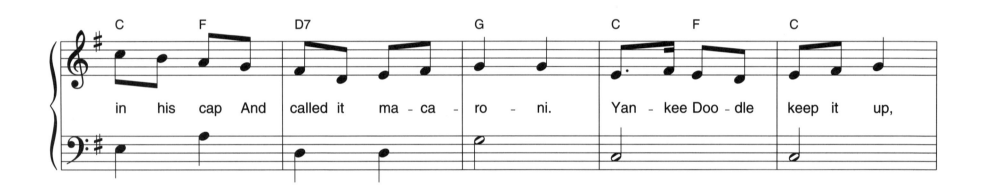

Tom, Tom, The Piper's Son

Tom, Tom, the piper's son,
Stole a pig and away did run;
The pig was eat, and Tom was beat,
And Tom went howling down the street.

A long time ago, people at markets and fairs used to sell sweet mince pies in the shape of pigs.

Three Little Kittens, They Lost Their Mittens

1. Three little kittens, they lost their mittens,
   So they began to cry,
   "O mother dear, come here, come here,
   For we have lost our mittens."
   "What, lost your mittens? You naughty kittens!
   Then you shall have no pie."
   "Mee-ow! Mee-ow!
   We shall have no pie."

2. Three little kittens, they found their mittens,
   So they began to cry,
   "O mother dear, come here, come here,
   For we have found our mittens."
   "Found your mittens? You good little kittens!
   Then you shall have some pie."
   "Purrrr! Purrrr!
   We shall have some pie."

Sing A Song Of Sixpence

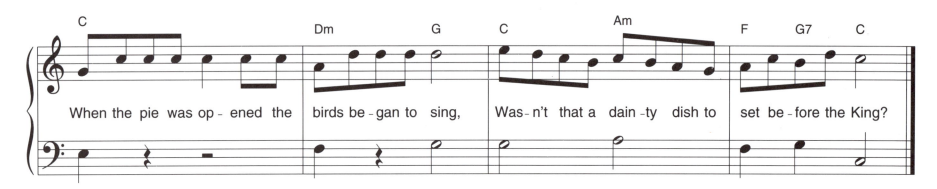

1. Sing a song of sixpence, a pocket full of rye,
   Four and twenty blackbirds baked in a pie.
   When the pie was opened the birds began to sing,
   Wasn't that a dainty dish to set before the King?

2. The King was in his counting house, counting out his money,
   The Queen was in the parlour, eating bread and honey,
   The maid was in the garden, hanging out the clothes,
   When down came a blackbird and pecked off her nose.

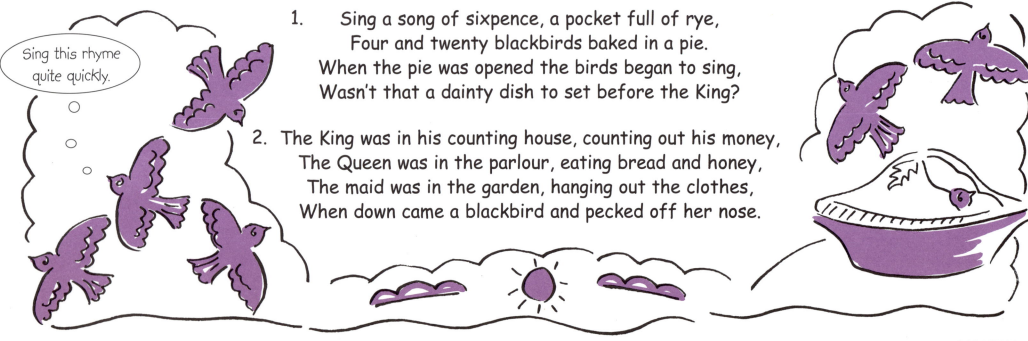

Sing this rhyme quite quickly.